Upon This Rock

*Marguerite Brunswig Staude
and her Sedona Chapel*

**by
Kate Ruland-Thorne**

Credits

by KATE RULAND-THORNE
Editor – Aliza Caillou
Cover Design – Dave Jenney
Cover Photography © 2003 by Jerry Sieve
Interior Design – Ron Henry
Publisher – Chapel of the Holy Cross
Historic Photographs – Courtesy of Tony Staude,
Fred Coukos and Fran Zimmer
Photograph – "THE CORPUS" (page 54)
By Bob Bradshaw

This book is distributed exclusively by
CHAPEL OF THE HOLY CROSS
A Roman Catholic Chapel
All inquiries should be addressed to
Chapel of the Holy Cross
780 Chapel Road
Sedona, Arizona 86336
Phone (928) 282-4069
this book can also be purchased from our Website
www.chapeloftheholycross.com

Acknowledgements

The author wishes to express her pleasure and sincere appreciation to Deacon Bob Anderson and to Tony Staude for allowing her the privilege of telling the story of how this wondrous Chapel came to be, and the remarkable woman who conceived the idea and carried it through to reality.

I also wish to thank Fred Coukos, Tony Staude and Fran Zimmer for sharing their insights and anecdotes which added so much flavor to already delightful project.

Kate Ruland-Thorne
Sedona, Arizona
September 11, 1995

Table of Contents

Chapter One

The Dream

Viewed from a distance, the Chapel of the Holy Cross seems to float like a dreamy vision, unattached to its red rock setting. Perched atop a 200 foot spur of rock seven miles south of the city of Sedona, one first glimpses it from State Highway 179 as it winds its way toward town. For many it's an ethereal apparition, equally astonishing as the magnificent red rock spires for which Sedona has become so famous.

Shortly after the Chapel's completion in 1956, the editor of *The Architectural Record* wrote:

"The Chapel does not seem bothered by the problem of scale. It does not feel called upon to feign modesty or bow to the hills in feeble imitation. Nor does it try self-assertiveness in the manner of a bantam rooster. Rather it seems to appreciate its magnificent setting and react to it like a well-mannered guest."

For the remarkable woman who conceived the idea of the Chapel of the Holy Cross and brought it to reality, this was indeed a rewarding commentary. Marguerite Brunswig Staude was studying art in New York City in 1932 when the idea for the Chapel of the Holy Cross first came to her.

"It was the beginning of Lent," she recalled. "All of New York seemed to have congregated at St. Patrick's Cathedral to receive the ashes. I, too, with their seal upon my brow, was heading my way out of the great Gothic portals facing Rockefeller Center which speaks so forcibly of today. At that moment, I could not help but wonder why the Church continued to cling to its past glory while seeming to totally ignore the present as if it did not exist. After all, do we not have contemporary language by which to worship? Gothic is fine, but Modern Gothic speaks, or may I say, sings so loudly today.

"These were my thoughts as I headed out among the great modern structures of Rockefeller Center. Can there be no church built to speak in contemporary language and provide an opening into liturgical arts?"

Marguerite continued down The Avenues toward her penthouse apartment on 85th Street with her mind intent upon these questions. As her eyes absorbed all the new structures which she passed, suddenly there was the Empire State Building, then under construction.

Emerging from its scaffolding, she saw a cross taking its form where the major vertical beam deliberately crossed the horizontal. Ah, she thought. Just as the Gothic spirit overrides matter...this is the hidden strength it carries behind its own structure.

The thought thrilled her and she said, "after entering my apartment, I was struck by the views of this same "Church." It was like a dream, now a vision from afar. It was an image which would haunt me until it became a realty.

But the idea did not take fire until after Marguerite returned to her studio in California and composed a sketch which she later showed to Lloyd Wright, son of Frank. He liked it.

"As a project, we agreed to work out a model architecturally," she said. "Lloyd promised to respect my sculptural form, so we worked at this project together for a full year. We scanned plans of Gothic Cathedrals and searched for a way to bring the modern back to the classic background from whence it came."

Within a few months, their cruciform church emerged. It involved a perforated doubled wall in tiny cement crosses. The whole structure would be lined with glass and the building would be done to a five hundred foot scale. It formed its own natural beacon for airplanes as it soared into space from four angles.

The main entrance was to hold the Mystic Emblem of Christ. Other inner cloisters contained Our Lady's Chapel, The Chapel of the Old Law and the Chapel of the New Testament. The altar, in the church, was also cruciform following the basic form of the entire structure.

"It was a most gratifying job during this time of the Depression," said Marguerite. "We hoped to build it around a square block in Los Angeles which was owned by the Catholic Church for its Cathedral of the Future.'"

But, alas, Marguerite and Lloyd Wright were ahead of their time. The Archbishop, though intrigued, could not quite understand this type of architecture, so he rejected their concept. It was simply too futuristic for him.

[2]

But in 1937, their plans were accepted by an order of nuns in Budapest, Hungary. It was to be built on Mount Ghelert which overlooks the Danube. Then World War II broke out in Europe, and the idea was abandoned. Marguerite's ambitious concept of a cruciform church was shelved for another twenty-five years.

In 1938, Marguerite met Tony Staude, the man who would become her life-long companion. Tony was an aspiring writer at the time. He worked in a men's store in Los Angeles to support himself while writing magazine articles about interesting Texans from his home town of Fort Worth.

One of those relocated Texans was Jake Zeitlin who had made a name for himself by opening a bookstore which was the gathering place for famous writers. In Jake's back room, he also sponsored art exhibitions.

Tony went to Jake's bookstore to interview him. During the interview, Jake showed him a bust of himself that had been sculpted by an artist named Marguerite Brunswig. He suggested Tony meet her and include her in his article.

A meeting was arranged the following week, but Marguerite did not show up. Tony dismissed the oversight and went on writing his story. About a week after that, Marguerite called him. She was very embarrassed and apologized for forgetting their meeting and hoped he would come to her home.

Already intrigued by her fascinating voice, Tony agreed to meet with her. Their first meeting remains as vividly imprinted on his mind as if it took place yesterday.

"She was fascinating to look at," recalled Tony. "Her movements were graceful, she had a beautiful smile and was warm and unaffected by the obvious wealth that surrounded her. She led me to her studio, which was at the bottom of the garden, completely separate from the formal mansion which was her home.

"I was immediately impressed with her art and her artistic concepts. Her work was very contemporary. For instance, she thought of trees as human and even had sculpted them with human attributes. I'd never been around any one like her. There was nothing about her that was snobbish. In fact it was quite clear she was more impressed with what people did with their lives than who their parents were.

"We shared so many ideas about art and literature that we ended up talking until after one in the morning. Needless to say, it was love at first sight."

Tony and Marguerite began dating immediately and within months, knew they wanted to marry. Tony met Marguerite's parents, who she referred to as Madame et Monsieur.

Both were skeptical about this young man their daughter seemed so enamored with. For one thing, Tony was not a Catholic and for another, his last name was not Rockefeller or Vanderbilt.

But Marguerite, always a determined woman, finally persuaded her parents to approve their marriage, and a small garden wedding was arranged at the family mansion. Monsieur, still skeptical, attended the ceremony in his bathrobe, complaining that he didn't feel well. Marguerite, seeing through his little charade, ignored it. Eventually, both Monsieur and Madame became good friends with their new son-in-law.

For some time, Madame had been concerned about the family's wholesale drug business. She knew it was in trouble. Even though her husband, now in his eighties, went to the office for a few hours each day, he was not actively involved in the everyday business. Although it was the time of the Great Depression, when all businesses were suffering, Madame, nevertheless, was certain that something more was wrong then met the eye.

Knowing Tony had a business background, she urged him to join the firm. Monsieur introduced him to all the executives in his company. Apparently Tony passed these tests and was accepted into the firm as a bookkeeper. It would become a sacrifice for Tony to join the firm because it meant giving up his aspirations of being a writer.

As the Brunswig Wholesale Drug Company once again prospered, the Staude's lives became full and happy. Their social life revolved around the cultural and art circles of Los Angeles where Marguerite had already made a name for herself as a sculptor.

After the United States became embroiled in World War II, Marguerite devoted herself to teaching clay modeling, as therapy, to wounded soldiers and blind people.

Then in 1941, they purchased a ranch in Sedona, Arizona. "Marguerite and I purchased the Doodlebug Ranch in Sedona," said Tony, "as a refuge from Los Angeles should the Japanese attack the West Coast. This refuge was encouraged by Madame who became alarmed after discussions with a friend close to a Kansas newspaper editor who believed in this possibility."

The Doodlebug Ranch became not only a refuge for the Staudes, but would remain their vacation retreat for the next twenty years.

In the 1940s, Marguerite (right) taught the blind ceramics.

Chapter Two

The Dream is Revived and Becomes a Reality

There was no church of any kind in Sedona in 1941. Services, including an occasional Mass, were held at the Brewer School, which then was a one-room school house. In those days, all Sedona consisted of was a grocery store, a bar, a filling station, a garage and a post office.

As Marguerite watched Sedona grow, she became obsessed with the idea for a Catholic Church. The idea continued to germinate and she even discussed it with several architects she knew, none of whom were residents of Sedona.

By 1946, both of Marguerite's parents had died; Lucien in 1943 and Madame in 1946. After their deaths, a patrimony was established for a memorial in their name.

"It was my mother's last wish," said Marguerite, "that she not die without fulfilling a living spiritual trust. That is when I decided to build a Chapel in their memory, in the name and the form of the cross.

"Tony and I had come to love Sedona, and we decided that we would build our memorial Chapel here in this red rock desert. Instead of a Cathedral, our monument would become a Chapel dedicated to finding God through art."

By 1950, Marguerite had discovered an unusual chapel in France which had been designed by the painter Roualt, for the purpose of finding God through art. She was captivated by this liturgical theme and realized that it was the very concept she was searching for. After returning to Los Angeles, she immediately contacted Lloyd Wright.

"We urged and pleaded with him to work with us on our new idea," she said, "but he refused, and clung to the original plans. But these plans were now beyond our reach financially."

[7]

Then one day, Marguerite was thumbing through a magazine and came across an extraordinary house built in Mexico. Its design intrigued her. She read that the architects, Anshen and Allen, were located in San Francisco. She and Tony met with them and the architects were immediately interested.

"After I explained my ideas to them, they were ready to be committed," said Marguerite "Our pact was sealed. There were four members of our committee, Tony, myself and the architects. We became much like a group of faithful following our theme."

The architects flew to Sedona and stayed with the Staudes at their Doodlebug Ranch. Together they began scouring the countryside looking for a suitable site. They went by foot, by jeep and by air. Flying terrified Marguerite who had never flown before.

"Although it was 1955, I had never braved the air," she said. "But for such a high purpose, I decided one need not fear. Before we knew it, the desert stretched out before us and we surveyed many possible sites by this means. I was relieved when we were finally able to step into the car and examine the sites which had presented themselves to us from the air."

Though the possibilities were infinite, there was really only one site which cut itself into space. It was a spur of rock which projected two-hundred feet above the desert floor. Two strange and significant discoveries followed which convinced the Staudes they had chosen the right place.

One was an RX, the apothecary emblem, which had been painted in the rocks at the foot of the spur. It was the very emblem which was to back the whole project. Also, as Marguerite stood on this pinnacle and looked northeast, she saw the Madonna and Child, carved by nature into its nearly perfect form.

"Yes, this was our site," she said. "Now we were set, all but for permits from Church and State."

She soon discovered that this was not going to be such an easy task. The site belonged to the Forest Service.

First she went to the local forestry office and was told they did not have the authority to even consider it. She was referred to their Flagstaff office. That office had the same reaction. They sent her to their regional office in Albuquerque where she heard the same thing again. That left only Washington, D.C., their national headquarters.

"Marguerite was a determined lady," said Tony. "We had met Barry Goldwater at a dinner party while he was in the Air Force and visiting L.A.. We saw him several times after that. By 1955, he was a Senator from Arizona. Marguerite flew to Washington,

*1955 - Everyone gathers for the ground breaking ceremonies.
Marguerite stands in the middle wearing her broad-brimmed hat.*

D.C. and met with him. After she explained the project and showed him the rendering, he was interested and convinced it should be built. He marched Marguerite over to the office of the Secretary of the Interior, who was immediately available. Inspired by Goldwater's enthusiasm, the Secretary of the Interior granted the necessary permit."

The next hurdle was receiving permission from the diocese of Arizona which was then located in Gallup, New Mexico. Bishop Espelage was in charge.

"Bishop Espelage reluctantly approved of the plans," said Tony. "He asked on many occasions why we would want to build such a strange looking church when the money could be put to better use for his Indians. Of course, that was not Marguerite's idea at all."

Marguerite (left) looks over a culvert for a retaining wall during construction.

Finally with all the permits granted, the Staudes chose the William-Simpson Construction Company of California to build it. The Brunswig Drug Company had already used them for several of their own projects, and although this was a much smaller structure than they were used to, they were enthusiastic about doing it.

In April of 1955, they broke ground. It took eighteen months to complete at a cost of $300,000, a modest sum even in those days. "The architects and the construction company cut their costs generously because they believed so wholeheartedly in the project," said Tony.

Six months after its completion, the dedication ceremony took place in the spring of 1957, with numerous people in attendance. "Many local people attended," said Tony, "along with the

Marguerite and Tony Staude with Father Driscoll (left)
prior to ground breaking ceremonies.

architects, the artists whose work was chosen to hang in the Chapel; the executives from the William-Simpson Construction Company and many of our friends from California. Father Driscoll presided.

"Carrying a large cross, he led the procession from the parking lot up the ramp, accompanied by a Monsignor from Phoenix. They were followed by twenty members of the Knights of Columbus, each decked out in their official regalia. Marguerite and I were next in line accompanied by our special guests.

"The Chapel was jammed with many people standing outside. Afterwards, everyone was invited to the Doodlebug Ranch for a barbeque. It was a most memorable day for all of us."

Within a year after it was completed, the Chapel had already garnered a great deal of publicity. It was featured in a LIFE MAGAZINE article, in THE NEW YORK TIMES and in the

*A Monsignor from Phoenix presides over
ground breaking ceremonies.*

WASHINGTON POST as well as in numerous architectural magazines. In 1956, it was given the prestigious AIA National Award for religious structures.

After the LIFE MAGAZINE article was published in 1956, the photographer Roger Sturtevant wrote to a friend: "It was a dividend to me to see such beauty, feel this happiness in the job. It was also an intellectual thrill for me to be so enthralled by a job whose basic design factors I would normally deplore. Like many visitors, I too wondered how on earth they ever built it. It was a job that was well nigh perfection. I feel it is one of the truly great architectural things in the world."

Well, how did they build it? Tony Staude gives a great deal of credit to the William-Simpson Company for selecting as their building superintendent, Fred Coukos.

Marguerite with architects Bob Anshen and Steve Allen.

Fred Coukos at the 1957 dedication ceremony.

Construction superintendent, Fred Coukos,
studies site prior to construction.

View from road looking toward site.

Chapter Three

Fred H. Coukos and his Daunting Construction Challenges

It was a cool morning in June 1995 when Fred Coukos sat in the shade of the Chapel entrance and recalled with pride his role as construction supervisor for the Chapel of the Holy Cross, 40 years before.

"I drove out here from California with my little dog Cookie," he said. "With me were the set of plans and specifications for the Chapel. There was no road to the site then, only rough car paths. In fact, there was nothing out here at all.

"To tell you the truth," Fred continued, "when I first set eyes on this site, I almost turned around and went home. It looked like too much of a challenge. But I quickly got over that. It turned out to be such an interesting job, that I felt privileged to have been picked to do it."

The William-Simpson Construction Company of Los Angeles, Fred's employer, had been chosen by the Staudes to build the Chapel because they had confidence in their ability.

"C.C. Simpson and his son, Collin, Jr. came to Sedona to view the site before agreeing to do it," recalled Tony Staude. "This was a much smaller project than they were used to, but the site and the architecture fascinated them. They could see that it would be a harrowing and difficult task that required the right person to oversee it. Fred had been with them for a number of years and proved many times his ability to tackle difficult jobs. So, they chose him as construction supervisor and in my opinion, they chose the right man for this daunting task."

Since early childhood, Fred Coukos had often faced difficult challenges. Born in Lynn, Massachusetts, the fourth of seven

Site location for Chapel prior to construction.

First step was to build retaining walls in order to hold soil for work area (now parking lot).

Batter boards are built for footing layout.

children, Fred's parents were Greek immigrants who were hard working and very strict.

"I was expected to work from the time I was able to walk," remembered Fred. "My father was a small contractor and took me on the job with him from the time I was little. I was told to pick up nails, straighten them, and as I got older, clean up the construction sites and do rough carpentry work. I always felt my dad was taking advantage of me. So when I was fifteen, I left home and went to work as a carpenter for another contractor."

By age 22, World War II had broken out and Fred spent four and a half years serving in the Army, six months of which were spent in the European conflict. After his honorable discharge from that service, he went to a hardware store and bought himself a hammer, level and saw and promptly went back to work as a carpenter. Three months later, he was made a foreman.

Solid rock was chipped out in order to provide area for stairs to basement of Chapel.

"I really thought I was a big shot then," laughed Fred. "Unfortunately my dad was no longer around when I finally supervised my first million dollar job."

Fred worked his way up the ladder through two major construction companies before finally joining the William-Simpson Company. He remodeled the Cedars of Lebanon Hospital for them and constructed two high rise buildings, as well as doing work on the Rand Corporation building in Santa Monica, California.

"I left that job to come out here in 1954," said Fred. "Of course I took one look at this site and thought, hell, I better get out of here before I screw something up."

Fortunately for everyone, Fred stayed, moving his family to Sedona, including his in-laws. "My family really liked it here," continued Fred. "My father-in-law went to work for me as a

Side view of solid rock chipped out for basement and stairs.

Batter boards constructed for layout of Chapel footings.

Batter boards and scaffolding for layout, and rock excavation for cross-footing.

carpenter, and when my wife's brother-in-law Bud Morris brought his family for a two week vacation, I told him hell, you're going to work. He was an excellent craftsman and I needed one. So he spent his vacation working on the Chapel, and I haven't heard the last of that yet. My wife Lucille did all our paper work from bookkeeping and paymaster to purchasing agent. I also was very pleased when the William-Simpson Company sent Carl Erickson out here to work as my foreman.

"My son and daughter went to the Brewer Elementary School and were in a classroom with the first through eighth grades. I'd guess the population of Sedona then was about 800 people. Sedona was a real country experience for us after living in Van Nuys, California."

Several weeks after the family arrived, Fred met the Staudes for the first time. "I really liked them," he said. "Marguerite told

Form work for ramp entrance constructed while work on the Chapel progresses.

me what she wanted, but after that, never butted in. They were easy to work for and we got along well. Marguerite was an all together different kind of person than I was used to being around...very artistic and cultured. She was elegant and nice. So was Tony. I knew I had to watch our costs pretty close, but cutting into those rocks took a lot more time and money than any of us figured."

"Fred faced many difficulties during construction," adds Tony Staude, "including trying to find the right workmen who were willing to risk their lives. There were a number of instances during the project when men refused to perform a task and it fell on Fred's shoulders to see it through."

Fred dismissed the dangers. "I was used to high rise work," he said. "Other than a few minor cuts and sprains, we had no serious accidents. The site was too small to hire a large crew, so I added to my crew as the work progressed."

Form work for upper portion of ramp.

Tower is constructed for hoisting lumber, concrete and other building materials. The concrete was raised by bucket up the tower and dumped in a hopper, then buggied to Chapel forms.

Forms being built for Chapel walls at the basement level. The twelve inch thick walls were made with reinforced concrete.

At the peak of construction, Fred had ten laborers and ten craftsmen working at the same time. Because the William-Simpson Company is located in California, a union state, he was required to hire union workmen for the job. Since Arizona is a non-union state, Fred imported many of his carpenters from L.A. while most of his laborers belonged to a union in Flagstaff.

"The first thing we did was put in the retaining walls below the present parking lot and brought up soil to create a working area for ourselves," said Fred. "The present parking lot, just below the Chapel, became our work area. After we got our work area established, I put a ladder up the rock face so the men could climb up to the Chapel's plaza level to work. There were large mounds of rock in the plaza area which had to be removed. After the mounds were broken up with pavement breakers, a bull dozer

View of 3rd lift. Side walls of Chapel were poured in a series of lifts. From 8 to 10 feet of concrete was poured for each lift.

View of sixth lift. Concrete required three days to set between pours. Note canvas covering used to protect fresh concrete during cold months. Also note two smudge pots set up along scaffolding.

*Opposite view of walls under construction. The finished walls
were sandblasted to expose the aggregate from the Verde River.*

was hauled from the west side of the Chapel area by tying it to a
cable attached to a dozer located on the east side of the Chapel
area. Tom Mulcaire, the excavating contractor, did the earth
moving. He also did all the road work including the culverts and
rock moving. What a daredevil he was."

For the next six weeks, four workmen chipped away at solid
rock. "The way we cut into the rock without dynamiting it was by
drilling a series of holes into the rocks and then chipping away
with pavement breakers and special steel chisels. About twenty-
five tons of rock was removed in this manner. We tried very hard
not to disturb the natural contours of this beautiful site."

While workmen chipped rocks, Fred set to work laying out the
ramp which winds its way from the parking lot to the Chapel
entrance. "I'd say the ramp was my biggest challenge, " he said.
"I had to put a lot of thought into shaping it around the existing

Front views of sixth lift before roof is poured.

Roof consisted of two slabs of concrete, one a structural slab separated by a membrane with a three inch slab on top, but not anchored

Form work for ramp.

rock formations and one of my workmen, Silver Gaddis, really helped me with the layout. The architect's plans were excellent, though, which really helped. They were the ones who did most of the hard thinking."

Once the rocks were chipped out, footings were created and a wooden tower was erected. As the Chapel went up, so did the runways.

Then it came time to sandblast and Tony remembers that nowhere in Arizona could Fred find the proper consistency of silica sand needed for sandblasting the surfaces of the Chapel and ramp in order to expose the aggregate. "He ended up having tons and tons of sand hauled from a beach in California."

"We needed a special silica sand for sandblasting," explained Fred. "I checked out the sand at Arizona's meteorite area but it

Diane Coukos, age 13, poses in her new squaw dress on ramp before her father's workmen pour concrete. Diane and her husband are now retired Verde Valley residents.

was not pure enough. So, we had sand delivered from a beach in Monterey, California, which was packed in seventy-five pound sacks."

Fred would have to draw upon his ingenuity numerous other times throughout the project. He couldn't just pick up a phone and have something he needed delivered to the site, as he was used to doing in L.A. There simply were no businesses in Sedona which could accommodate him. As a result, Fred became very inventive.

"There was no electricity at the site and no water. I couldn't purchase ready-mix concrete either. Everything had to be hauled. A generator provided our electricity and we mixed our own concrete at the site. Ed Starkey, who owned the sand and gravel business we used, hauled over 500 yards of aggregate for us making at least one hundred trips in his little bob tail truck. The sand and gravel he hauled came from the Verde River below

Retaining walls for parking area. At lower left the runway was raised to roof level with concrete hopper in place for roof pour.

Clarkdale. On one occasion, while they were digging, they uncovered the remains of a pre-historic Indian woman who still wore her shell bracelet and buckskin dress."

Another great challenge was the dramatic changes in temperature, particularly during the winter months. Freezing temperatures often caused delays in pouring the concrete. Fred tried protecting the freshly poured concrete by draping layers of canvas over it. Finally he rented smudge pots from Walter Jordan who owned orchards in Sedona, and solved the problem that way.

Lucille, Fred's wife, felt sorry for the workmen during the cold months and one day incurred her husband's wrath by bringing up steaming containers of coffee and home made donuts. Everyone stopped work and enjoyed this treat, but Fred was annoyed with her. He didn't like anything interrupting the work. He now recalls that day, and others, with humor.

Forms removed three days after concrete is poured. Sandblasting took place immediately after removal of forms.

"Priests and nuns, visiting from other places, often came up here to watch our progress," said Fred. "One time, I was really cussing out a workman who had made a big mistake. When I turned around, there was a priest standing behind me. I was embarrassed and really apologized to him. He said, don't worry about it. I was a chaplain in the Navy for years and heard a lot worse than that.'"

Fred also laughed about another incident when Father Driscoll handed him a sack of holy medals and told him to scatter them in the concrete as it was being poured. "I'm not Catholic," said Fred, "so I handed the sack to Frenchy, one of my Catholic workmen. Man, he thought he'd been given some holy order. He's definitely going to heaven now, you know. It meant a hell of a lot to the guy."

Lower half of ramp completed while roof of Chapel was being poured. Note retaining walls below parking lot and Fred's 53 Chevy truck which was used to haul gasoline for generator, hoist and water pumps.

As the weather began to warm, Father Driscoll decided to hold mass outside at the foot of the Chapel's cross and asked Fred to construct a temporary altar for him. "The turnout was great every Sunday," recalled Fred, "but people soon brought their own pillows to kneel on while trying to ignore the ants. No one complained. Many even said they had never felt closer to God."

After the Chapel was completed, a number of cracks developed in the large plate-glass window behind the altar. The Pittsburgh Glass Company had manufactured the plate glass which was called Duscolite. It was beautiful to look at, but according to Tony, did not hold up under Sedona's extreme temperatures.

View of lower ramp and work area.

"Through the William-Simpson Company, we were able to contact the higher echelons of management in Pittsburgh," said Tony. "They were very proud that their glass had been used at the Chapel because by then, the Chapel had garnered a lot of national recognition. They were most cooperative and sent their engineers out. The engineers went back to Pittsburgh and developed a special glass just for the Chapel and replaced it with the original. Afterwards, there were no more cracks caused by temperature, but a few have happened since, because of aircraft exceeding the sound barrier."

As Fred reminisced about the construction of the Chapel, he pointed to a little cedar tree growing alongside the upper ramp. "You can thank me for that tree," he said. "It was just a few feet tall forty years ago. I nursed it along and protected it from being destroyed. I'm kinda proud of that."

Fred Coukos is proud of all he accomplished regarding the

Fred stands proudly with Marguerite Staude after Chapel is completed. The Chapel took 18 months from start to finish.

Chapel of the Holy Cross. "I never expected this Chapel to be so popular," he says. "It was just supposed to be a little Chapel. But it is kind of unique. As far as construction goes, well it wasn't that tough, really, and I had a terrific crew working for me. But I do think we get a lot more credit for it than we deserve."

Tony Staude would not agree. He gives a great deal of credit to Fred and his crew. It was Tony who conceived the idea of having the Chapel's history finally told in detail because so many people have asked about it. The two questions asked most often are: how was this unusual structure actually built, and just who was Marguerite Brunswig Staude?

Marguerite, who gave the Chapel to Sedona as a memorial to her parents, was a product of her times and her upbringing. Had she been born to different parents in another era and under dissimilar circumstances, Sedona's Chapel of the Holy Cross would never have come to be.

[33]

Fred Coukos in 1995 with "his" little cedar tree.

*We must look upon this Chapel as an embodiment of the artistic
and soul-searching efforts of our fellow man. We may rejoice
that we can accept or reject and certainly pass judgment.
Few will be without an opinion. This is a healthy attitude and
Sedona is fortunate in having this Chapel in its midst*

By Ed Ellinger
Arizona Highways, 1957.

Chapter Four

From the Gilded Age to the Gilded Cage

The Life and Times of Marguerite Brunswig Staude

Marguerite Brunswig Staude was born in New Orleans, Louisiana, on November 9, 1899. That year would mark the end of an era known as the "Gilded Age," a time remembered for its profound industrial growth and westward expansion. It also had been an age when wealth, lineage and social standing was idolized.

Her parents, Lucien and Marguerite Brunswig, belonged to America's privileged class, but their daughter did not always share their enthusiasm for it. When she came of an age to be presented to society as a debutante, they were shocked when she announced she would rather become an artist.

In her struggle to establish her own identity, Marguerite sometimes conflicted with her doting parents, but the conflicts never developed into rifts. The three remained entirely devoted to one another throughout their lives.

Her parents affectionately called their daughter "Madole," a name Marguerite gave herself when she was small because she was unable to pronounce her own name. Whenever she referred to them, it was as "Madame et Monsieur."

In the 1860s, Marguerite's father Lucien Brunswig, immigrated to the United States with his parents from Montmedy, France. This was an era of overwhelming European migration initiated by America's Homestead Act of 1862. The Act provided that any adult citizen (or ones intending to become citizens) who headed a family could qualify for a grant of 160 acres of public land by paying a small registration fee and living on the land continuously for five years. The government's incentive was to populate as much of the vast and vacant stretches of land west of the Mississippi River as possible.

Although only a teenager at the time, Lucien Brunswig already had been trained in pharmaceuticals. After his family settled in Topeka, Kansas, he became an apprentice in a pharmacy.

Frugal and enterprising, Lucien saved enough money to follow the Southern Pacific and Santa Fe Railroad to its new terminus in the little frontier town of Ft. Worth, Texas. At the time of the Civil War, railroads were already a fixture in the Eastern United States. After the war, railroads would change the future of America forever.

As America became more determined than ever to expand toward the West, railroads served this expansion faster and more efficiently than any other mode of transportation. In fact the railroads created the West by transporting the waves of immigrants, attracted by the Homestead Act, to settle in the western spaces they served.

Lucien Brunswig, alert to the economic stimulus created by these transportation hubs, was among those enterprising immigrants who realized that wherever a railroad established a terminus, towns, cities and businesses soon flourished and prospered. He opened his first small pharmacy in 1882, on Houston Street in Ft. Worth, Texas. With this modest beginning, he set himself upon the path of the American Dream.

Five years later, Lucien sought a larger metropolitan city in which to expand his interests. By 1887, he was married with four children. That same year he settled in New Orleans with his family, and purchased an interest in the Findley Wholesale Drug Company which became Findley and Brunswig. This move had also been prompted by railroad activities.

The mushroom growth of this new transportation system following the Civil War had all but killed the steamboat trade on the Mississippi River. With the coming of the railways in 1882, Louisiana enjoyed a new prosperity with the large-scale production of rice, and New Orleans had become its transportation center.

Several years after moving his family to this bustling city, Lucien's young wife died. Following a discreet period of mourning, Lucien entered the active and colorful social life of the City of the Mardi Gras. It was here that he met and fell in love with the beautiful Marguerite Wogan.

[42]

Madame Wogan was one of New Orleans' most eligible society matrons. A widow herself, Madame was a member of a distinguished French Creole family on her mother's side.

Her mother's family were wealthy plantation owners who fled French owned Haiti in 1802, during a devastating slave revolt, barely escaping with their lives. They and other French refugees were encouraged by Emperor Napoleon to relocate in New Orleans, a predominantly French city, which had been founded by French Canadians in 1718.

For 45 years after its founding, New Orleans and the Louisiana Territory were owned by France. Then, following a war with Spain, the territory was ceded to that country in 1763. By 1801, Spain had secretly ceded Louisiana back to France. By acquiring the Louisiana Territory, Napoleon hoped to expand his empire in North America. But the Haitian slave revolt of 1802 proved more costly than he anticipated and his impending war with England finally led him to abandon these plans.

This opened the door for President Thomas Jefferson to purchase all of the Louisiana Territory for 15 million dollars. For approximately four cents an acre, the United States acquired about 828,000 square miles. The eastern boundary of this territory was the Mississippi River; the Gulf of Mexico formed the southern boundary; the northern boundary reached all the way to Canada, and the Western boundary ran generally through present day Montana. The purchase of this long held foreign territory doubled the lands of the United States.

But despite America's new ownership of Louisiana and the lands beyond, New Orleans remained distinctly French and Spanish in character, language, religion, custom and culture. This fascinating cultural mix was the pure French "Creole" heritage of which Madam Wogan was extremely proud. She married Lucien in New Orleans in the 1890s, assuming they would always live in the beloved city of her birth. But it was not to be so.

Always perceptive about economic opportunities, Lucien had already considered the financial potential of yet another new railroad terminus, this time in Los Angeles, California, where the Santa Fe Railroad had again expanded in 1887. One year later, Lucien backed a Mr. F.W. Braun who established a wholesale drug firm in that city.

After his daughter Marguerite's birth in 1899, Lucien found buyers for his New Orleans investments and moved his family to Los Angeles. There he formed a partnership with F.W. Braun and opened a large wholesale drug company on Main Street, near the Los Angeles Mission.

[43]

Madame et Monsieur Brunswig, circa 1930s.

Marguerite Brunswig, age 6

Madame was aghast at the idea of moving so far from her family. She became even more horrified after they actually moved to Los Angeles in 1904.

By her standards, Los Angeles seemed a crude frontier town. Its population at the time was just under 50,000. Although founded as a mission outpost by Father Junipero Serra in 1781, 63 years after the founding of New Orleans, Los Angeles had not yet developed any of the elite cultural amenities nor acquired the sophistication which made New Orleans so "superior."

To Madame, Los Angeles was a hodgepodge of riff-raff and wild Indians. Not only was there no opera, no fancy balls nor special social activities to attend, she couldn't find anyone who spoke French. Adding insult to injury, the hotel they were living in burned to the ground and all of their possessions were destroyed.

Thoroughly distraught by all they had been through since their move, Madame gathered up her six year old daughter Marguerite and Marguerite's governess, Fraulein Gerstmeyer, and proceeded to travel abroad for the rest of the year. It was something she continued to do for a number of years afterwards. Whenever he could, Lucien joined them, taking advantage of the opportunity to visit his older children who now attended school in Switzerland.

Then in 1910, Lucien made a final effort to get his wife to stay in Los Angeles by building her a mansion on West Adams Boulevard. He modeled it after a French Chateau which rose two stories above five acres of lush ground. Indeed Madame loved it. She surrounded herself with friends, most of whom were European and intellectually stimulating. Numerous members of the clergy, particularly those with charming social graces and intellect, also were included at her dining table. In the early 1920s, she attended the concerts of the budding Los Angeles Symphony every Friday afternoon, and with her support, helped form the Alliance Francais, a school which offered studies in French literature and art.

Marguerite would spend the rest of her childhood at the family Chateau, and later, her vacations from finishing school at the Convent of the Sacred Heart in Menlo Park, California. She continued to travel to Europe with her mother, but now their visits were shorter.

Within this environment, which included stays in France and Italy, Marguerite became steeped in religious art and Catholicism. As a child she remembered one incident when she and her mother were granted an audience with the Pope in which he anointed her head. Later, when Fraulein Gerstmeyer tried to wash her hair,

Marguerite cried, "No, No, it will wash off the Pope's hand."

Growing up with art, Marguerite developed an almost innate craving for her own artistic expression. Another influence that possibly inspired her interests were the radical changes ushered in with the dawning of the Twentieth Century, particularly the changes in the arts.

Typically the arts mirror the spirit of the times, and at the time of Marguerite's birth, Americans were starting to travel in motorized vehicles and communicate across continents and oceans by telephone and telegraph. Sigmund Freud probed man's unknown inner being while Albert Einstein challenged our concepts of time and space.

Music, drama, painting, sculpture, architecture, literature and the dance also were transformed by this new era, encouraging numerous great innovators to emerge. Among them were Spanish painter Pablo Picasso and American architect Frank Lloyd Wright. In time, Marguerite would become intensely influenced by these innovators who contributed to her yearning to develop her own extraordinary talents as a sculptor.

Not surprisingly, Madame and Monsieur were dismayed when their brilliant and talented daughter told them that she had no interest in becoming a debutante and would rather study art abroad. Her father opposed the idea vehemently. Furthermore he did not believe that a young lady should live abroad without a chaperone. Entreaties were fruitless.

In the early 1930s, Marguerite devised a scheme: On Christmas Eve, gifts were being distributed in the drawing room. Everyone present was curious about one gift that had no recipient's name on it. It was a live canary in a gilded cage. Finally Marguerite stepped forward and gave the cage to her father. "For you, Monsieur," she said. Surprised, he frowned, then gradually smiled. He realized his daughter was depicting her plight...a bird in a gilded cage. At last he granted her permission to study art abroad. Choosing sculpture as her medium, Marguerite embarked upon an exciting quest, to study art with the finest teachers in Mexico City, Greece, Italy, Paris and finally New York City where she would conceive the idea of her now famous Chapel of the Holy Cross.

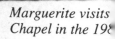

*Marguerite visits
Chapel in the 198*

Chapter Five

Remembering Marguerite Staude and the Chapel's Early Years

Marguerite Staude died on May 15, 1988, Fran Zimmer's birthday. Fran and Marguerite had become great friends over the years, often taking adventurous trips together and always having a memorable time. Their friendship began shortly after Fran moved to Sedona in 1963. It was a time when Sedona was just becoming of interest to tourists, and besides the red rocks, the Chapel was one of the town's few attractions.

"There was one art gallery in Sedona then," recalls Fran, "THE GALLERIA, (now Son Silver West) and the Sedona Arts Center had just gotten started in the Jordan apple packing barn. Sedona was only a little village, very different than it is today. It was a place where everyone knew one another and most of us gathered at Oma Bird's Oak Creek Tavern in uptown to socialize. But the Chapel was the main attraction. When I arrived there was just a rough dirt road leading up to it and by then the Chapel had become run down. But visiting priests did serve Mass there until St. John Vianney Church was established in 1965."

Shortly after Fran arrived in Sedona, she was asked to start a gift shop at the Chapel because visitors wanted a place where they could buy holy medals and souvenirs. Fran operated the gift shop, all by herself, for the next five years.

Since the Chapel was not in the best condition in 1963, people from the parish helped her clean it up. "I often worked until midnight," she recalls. "Since I was the only one there, I decided to live at the Chapel rather than go back and forth. In those days, there were just a few homes in the area, but I was too busy to become frightened about being there alone."

[49]

*Fran Zimmer and Marguerite Staude on one of their
frequent outings together.*

Every morning, Fran cleaned the Chapel inside and out before
opening the gift shop. She put chains on all the holy medals in
order to save money, and because she was the only person
working there, she put up signs to tell people what not to do.
"Mine were some of the most ignored signs in history," she
laughed.

"People often got beyond the altar railing, so I had a sign
asking them not to do that. When they did it anyway, they'd find
another sign that read "DIDN'T YOU READ THE SIGN THAT
SAID YOU WEREN'T SUPPOSED TO BE UP ON THE
ALTAR?

"There also was a contribution box, and once in a great while,
young people tried to remove dollar bills out of it when I wasn't
around. They'd put gum on the end of a stick and pull out the
dollars, so I wrote "GOD SEES YOU" on top of several dollar

bills inside the box. I don't think it stopped them. I kept everyone entertained by all my signs."

Fran also chuckles about an incident when a priest arrived early one morning and asked to borrow the Extreme Unction box. He told Fran he needed it in order to give another priest last rites. "He said this other priest had just had a heart attack, and he promised to bring the box back by noon.

"I'd never seen this priest before, but I believed him and loaned him the box. Noon came and went and he didn't return. By six that evening, I was worried. I called the headmaster of Brophy Prep School in Phoenix, where the priest said he was from, and asked about him. The priest there said that yes, he was a priest and the priest he went to administer to had died. I was so relieved, that without thinking I answered, oh, thank God."

Each morning, Fran scrambled around the rocks picking up debris left by visitors, most of which were beer bottles. "One nice little priest, who came up from Phoenix to offer Mass, always caught me picking up beer bottles and he loved to say, I wish you wouldn't drink so much."

Masses were held at the Chapel on a regular basis until 1974. On an irregular basis, a variety of programs also took place. There were Easter festivals, Thanksgiving festivals, Midnight Masses at Christmas time, poetry readings, art exhibits and dance and theater programs.

The most stunning program of all, however, occurred in 1965 when the Columbia Broadcasting Company filmed a Christmas special at the Chapel entitled "GO TELL IT ON THE MOUNTAIN." It starred folk singers Chad Mitchell and Judy Collins.

The producer-director, Chalmers Dale, was a gifted young man who had risen from shipping clerk to producer after 15 years with CBS. He had traveled all over this country and Europe in search of a suitable setting for this special production, finally deciding upon Sedona and the Chapel of the Holy Cross. Fran remembers the production well.

"It took a week for them to film it," she said. "In those days, all of our water had to be hauled up to the Chapel in a truck. There was quite a crew here for the filming. The director asked me to fix coffee for everyone one morning. I don't drink coffee so I don't make it very well. We were so low on water that morning that the coffee they got was too strong to drink. I wasn't asked to do that again," she laughed. "It turned out to be a very special broadcast and CBS ran it at Christmas time for three or four years afterwards."

Fran Zimmer at Chapel in 1960s

*On May 15, 1995 Fran Zimmer was honored by the Chapel and
the City of Sedona for her 25 years of community service.
Referring to her as Sedona's champion volunteer, Deacon Bob
Anderson said in his speech: "We know now that the Chapel
would not have become what it is today without you."*

But of all her memories, Fran's friendship with Marguerite
Staude remains the most enduring.

"Marguerite was a sculptor, a personality and a character,"
recalls Fran. "There was no one else like her. Although she was
very religious, she never cow-towed to anyone. Marguerite knew
art and read a lot of books on philosophy. She reminded me of
Mrs. Payne Whitney. I liked the fact that she was a woman who
got things done. Once she made up her mind to do something, she
just did it. Her husband Tony was the only person I know of who
could say no to her and she'd listen. I found her very much to my
liking."

Marguerite and Fran took trips together. Fran's favorite memory was of the time they went to Santa Fe and Taos, New Mexico, in the late 1960s.

"We traveled by train. Marguerite had packed all of her belongings in straw baskets which she'd bought in Mexico. She wore a Mexican outfit with a big straw hat. I thought she looked stunning, but she told me that Tony would never allow her to travel with him looking like that.

"After we attended a retreat in Abiquiu near Santa Fe, we took a cab to Taos. We needed a place to stay. There was only one big old hotel in Taos in those days, but it was seedy looking and run down. There were creepy looking people hanging out in the lobby, too. But we had no choice. I scrubbed our room thoroughly before we went to bed. After we got home, I found out from a friend that we'd stayed in a brothel. I told Marguerite about it and she laughed. She said it wasn't the first time she'd stayed in a brothel.

"When she was nineteen, she told me that she and her mother were on one of their annual trips to Europe and needed some place to stay in London. Her mother sent her off to find a place and Marguerite discovered a beautiful old house that had been converted into a hotel, so she booked a suite of rooms. After she and her mother moved in, they called their friends to say where they were and their friends laughed. 'Oh, they said, the King Edward's Brothel?'

"Marguerite had a great sense of humor, but she could be rather austere at times as well. She loved filmy, casual clothes and big hats with sashes she could tie under her chin. In her own way she was quite fashionable. It never bothered her that some people found her different. She was not one to care what others thought.

"One time, when I visited the Staudes in California, we went to Bob Hope's home for a meeting. Marguerite wore a fabulous oriental outfit and looked absolutely stunning. She was a tall, rugged looking woman and I considered her quite handsome."

After the Chapel was built, Bishop Espelage of Gallup did not approve of the huge corpus which was installed over the altar. But Marguerite had commissioned artist Keith Monroe of San Francisco to design it, and she was not about to tell him it would not be hung. In time, that Corpus became nearly as famous as the Chapel itself.

But according to Fran, the intense controversy which continued to surround it, marred Marguerite's enjoyment of it, and she often worried that she had made a mistake by going against the Bishop's wishes.

©BOB BRADSHA

[54]

"Some people thought it was one of the most wonderful crucifixes they had ever seen," explained Fran, "because it depicted Christ's extreme sorrow and suffering. Others saw it as a desecration. I could see both sides."

Among comments written in the Chapel guest book regarding the corpus, the following were typical:

"The Chapel is beautiful. I also think the crucifix is beautiful because it gives me the feeling of the terrific agony Christ went through for us."

"The Corpus denies the resurrection of Our Redeemer. Christ's body was never in such a state of decay."

"The view around is beautiful, but not the Chapel. The cross is atrocious."

"Magnificent in concept and execution. A shrine to live in the heart of the wayfarer as long as the memory of this superb setting lives."

"As Marguerite thought about it over the years," continued Fran, "she reached a point where she felt she had built the Chapel more for the risen Christ, not the suffering one. That crucifix really gnawed at her over time."

Then in the early 1980s, the crucifix was removed. No one living today seems to know how, why or what happened, it simply disappeared and will remain a mystery which may never be resolved.

On Fran's birthday in 1988, Marguerite Brunswig Staude died of heart failure, just a few months before she and Tony would have celebrated their 50th wedding anniversary. Her memorial service was held at the Chapel. Since then, her husband has returned often to Sedona from their home in Big Sur, California.

Among the articles written about the Chapel which he and Marguerite had saved over the years, a New York Times article written on August 25, 1957, was perhaps Marguerite's favorite. It was accompanied by two large photos of the Chapel of the Holy Cross with the headline NEW CHURCHES ARE ANTICIPATING THE FUTURE INSTEAD OF REFLECTING THE PAST. Writer Glenn Fowler described several new church and synagogues structures, but placed his emphasis on Sedona's Chapel of the Holy Cross:

"Perhaps the most striking of some thirty-five churches and synagogues surveyed in the new book (RELIGIOUS

BUILDINGS FOR TODAY) is the Roman Catholic Chapel of the Holy Cross at Sedona, Arizona. It owes much of its awesomeness to the fact that it is perched on the spur of a cliff rising from the floor of the Verde Valley. When viewed from afar, the Chapel exposes a cross ninety feet high. accentuating the Christian symbol with a starkness that matches the ruggedness of the canyon around it. It represents the ultimate in fitting a structure to its site. It also indicates a trend, found particularly in Roman Catholic churches, toward designs markedly different from that of the traditional house of worship. "

Marguerite must have loved that final statement. After all, it had been her initial dream and concept in 1932, which helped inspire the changes in design of America's traditional Catholic structures. It is likely that the national recognition and architectural awards garnered by the Chapel of the Holy Cross, after it was built, were instrumental in awakening and inspiring these dramatic changes from Gothic to modern. Today, thousands of visitors each year make a pilgrimage to the Chapel of the Holy Cross. Regardless of their faith, most experience a sense of reverence after entering it. This was important to Marguerite. It was another of her dreams that the Chapel of the Holy Cross would be open to one and all regardless of creed. She once wrote: "May this church come to life in the souls of men and be a living reality...herein lies the whole message of this Chapel."

Among the many visitors who have returned time and again, John Dinwiddie, one of San Francisco's leading contractors, returned with his teenage son. After much thought, his son turned to him and asked, "But dad, it is Gothic, isn't it?" and his father replied: "Yes, son...in spirit."